"The highest of distinctions is service to others."

King George VI

LISTEN *UP,*
CUSTOMER SERVICE

The Game Has Changed

by David Cottrell
and Mark C. Layton

To order additional copies of
Listen Up, Customer Service!
The Game Has Changed
complete the order form found on page 43.

For information on CornerStone Leadership
products and services
call 1-888-789-LEAD or
visit www.cornerstoneleadership.com

CornerStone
Leadership Institute*

CornerStone Leadership Institute
P.O. Box 764087
Dallas, Texas 75376
888.789.LEAD

Printed in the United States of America
ISBN: 0-9658788-5-6

Cover design: ConceptFX
Book design: Precision Type

How to Get the Most Out of This Book!

U Read with a highlighter in your hand. Mark key words or phrases that pertain to your personal situation.

U After reading this book, take the CornerStone Customer Service Self-Test on pages 37-38.

U When you complete this book, order copies for everyone you know responsible for customer satisfaction.

CONTENTS

INTRODUCTION

It's a
whole new game!

*In business, the competition will
bite you if you keep running. If you
stand still, they will swallow you.*
— William Knudsen

Whatever the decade, whatever the Millennium...
customer service has always been the name of the
game...whether you were selling the first wheel in the
Stone Age or selling seats on the first commercial flight
to the moon in the not-too-distant future.

Think about it! Customers are the most important ingre-
dients to any company's success. Without them, nothing
else matters — without customers, executives, accounting,
marketing, maintenance and every other employee of
your company would have to find another place to work.

So, why do most customers choose to do business with you? Product quality plays an important part in the relationship, but outstanding customer service keeps 'em coming back for more. And even if you're selling the finest product of its kind, if customer service is lacking, good clients will eventually disappear.

Dollars lost due to poor customer service are seldomed tallied or reported, but estimates place these lost dollars in the millions each year.

> Service is the reason people choose to spend money with a certain company.

One more thought: Service is the reason people choose to continue to spend money with a certain company. Management allocates time and resources; customers dictate how much money will be available for management to allocate.

This book is written to help you take care of your customers in a way that will increase the resources available to your company.

Customer service slogans blanket the halls of almost every company: *Customers are First! We Exist to Serve the Customer! Think Customer! Customer Champions! 100% Customer Focus! The Customer is King! We are Customer Driven!* And on and on. While the slogans are nice and make great banners, many customers will tell you — if you ask them — that the two words, *customer and service*, are a dichotomy in many companies today.

The good news is that it does not have to be that way!

Most of the time customers are not unreasonable, stupid, or the idiots many customer service people describe them. But customers do have needs. They need to understand the alternatives, they need to be listened to, paid attention to, respected and they need to make decisions based on how well a product fill their needs. Does that sound unreasonable, stupid or idiotic?

People become your customer for many different reasons — new product ideas, marketing value and/or reputation. However, in most instances, people decide to do business with a particular company for one reason — customer service — how well they are treated.

Think about your own experiences. Would you be more likely to return to a restaurant with good service and a mediocre menu or a restaurant with a great menu with lousy service? Most people choose to not return to the restaurant with the great menu and bad service — who needs the hassle and stress?

Fair or not, people make the decision to become your customer, primarily, based on how well customer service does their job. Yes, customer service performance is even more important — in many instances — than the performance of the product.

I know because I am a customer. In fact, I might have been one of your most loyal customers for many years. But, today I am giving you fair warning... the selling and buying arena has changed.

In the past, I have chosen to be your customer, first of all, because you were one of the only alternatives available. Today, the game has changed — and you have to change as well if you are going to keep me as a client.

One of the changes in this new game is that I now have a lot more choices. You are no longer the only alternative. And you know what? I like having more choices. I think my decisions are better when I have more choices but, quite frankly, my risks are greater, too.

New winners will emerge from this exciting marketplace and, believe it or not, I want you to be one of those winners. That's why this book is loaded with tips on how you can keep earning the right to my business.

> This book is loaded with tips on how you can keep earning the right to my business.

This book will also tell you how to do more than just survive in the new game. It will supply you with a road map to create enormous success. Get ready for some straight talk from a customer who cares!

Stay in School

It's what you learn after you know

it all that counts.

—*John Wooden*

I know, you probably do not want to go back to school and I can hear you saying, "What more can I learn at my age — or at this point in my career?"

That is exactly my point. The best customer service people and the best companies are always willing to learn! I want to do business with people who keep up with the trends… people who want to be better than average…those who work at being *extraordinary* in what they do.

Becoming a student in the three schools listed below — where you never get too smart, too old, or too big to graduate — is an important first step. In fact, the people who think they don't need more education or information are the big losers in the business world today and I do not like to do business with losers! Stay enrolled in these schools.

The 'Voice of the Customer' School

For years studies have shown that customers leave companies for reasons that seldom have anything to do with product quality. Most customers will leave because they feel the chilly air of indifference toward them, or, in other words, the company does not care! Where are the roots of this attitude? They can generally be found in the most important ingredient to any company's success — their customer.

Your "nice" customers can absolutely kill your business. They can be so nice that they never complain. This makes it easy for you to make the assumption that everything is okay. Well, you know what they say about assumptions? Many of those "nice" customers fade without notice into

There's no point in complaining! Nothing will change!

the deadly category of ex-customers. In fact, studies have shown that only four percent of your customers will take time to complain. I guess the others think it's just not worth it. Why? Because they probably think nothing will change anyway, and who wants the confrontation and hassle?

Sometimes your nice customers could raise the issue and feel better, but they make the decision to just leave quietly. They take what is dished out because they know they are never coming back. Who could blame them?

To stay on top of customer satisfaction, you have to seek complaints and saturate your company with the voices of your customers! Yes, you read that right. Search and find complaints!

Seek complaints and saturate your company with the voices of your customers!

Okay, okay...I know what you may be saying: "Why should I do that? Hearing complaint after complaint is downright demoralizing?"

Hold that thought — because the reality is that for every complaint you hear without aggressively being involved in a complaint-seeking mission, there are at least 25 other people who chose not to complain...some of those "nice customers" we discussed earlier.

And, remember this: It is far more demoralizing to wake up at the end of the month with fewer customers than you thought you had and not know the reason why.

Complaints are good! Because the only way you can make positive change is to know what needs to be changed. As you seek complaints, you are also subtlety telling your customers that you care about them and their business. And, you'll find that taking the time to go through this thorny exercise will ultimately reward you with more customer tolerance and loyalty when things are not going well.

The 'School of Expertise and Passion'

Hear that buzz? It's your customer base pleading, "Please listen to me; you are my lifeline to good decisions. Become the absolute expert in your job and feel good

One of the key questions you have to ask — and answer — almost immediately is, "Would you buy from you?"

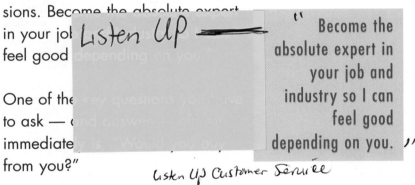

Listen Up ————

"Become the absolute expert in your job and industry so I can feel good depending on you."

Listen Up Customer Service

If you would feel good about buying from yourself, your customers probably would also. Remember, the way customers feel about doing business with you determines the amount they spend. The better we feel, the more we spend!

Hear that buzz again? It's your customer base saying, "The more you know about your products and the marketplace, the more confident I am in making the decision to do business with you."

"Your confidence is exhibited to me by your passion to service my needs. Your enthusiasm for serving me makes me more willing to give you my business. If you become an expert in the market and your products, you will know the answers to my questions before I even ask them. I like that!"

The 'School of Self-Development.'

Why do customers care about your self-development? Because most people enjoy doing business with people they like, and they like people who are always learning and improving.

> Because most people enjoy doing business with people they like, and they like people who are always learning and improving.

The more you read and educate yourself, the more you will be able to help your customers make better choices. The more you listen, the better you will be able to understand your customer's point of view. The more you improve in communication skills, the easier it will be for customers to understand your point of view. You see, self-development is a process that never ends. Things change. Always have. Always will. Unless you stay on top of these changes, you and I will both be left out.

> **Self-development is a process that never ends.**

Part of self-development is taking care of yourself. There comes a time when everybody needs a break. Don't feel bad about getting away. Allow one of your peers that you trust to take your responsibilities and go. If you allow burnout to creep in, we will both pay the price for it.

One more point: The result of you becoming a life-long student is that you will be able to ask the right questions, so listen to what I am telling you. Learn from other customers, recommend the appropriate product and tell me why this is the best decision for me. That makes it a good deal for both of us!

By the way, your customers are — or should be — life-long students, as well. Customers study what your competitors are doing. They listen to the best sales pitches and know their strengths and weaknesses. Want to know something else? Your customers could become real-world professors for you. Think about it!

A Customer's
Top Ten Service Attributes

1. Treat me with respect. I am a customer, not an account number.

2. Follow through on your commitments.

3. Communicate with me the good and the bad.

4. Talk to me without interruption.

5. Answer the phone quickly.

6. Provide alternatives when we have a problem.

7. Allow me to talk to someone in authority when there is a problem.

8. Clearly state what I should expect from you.

9. Know everything about your products and services.

10. Be a customer advocate.

Everything Counts

If things go wrong, don't go with them.

—*Roger Babson*

The customer service experience begins when a customer — any customer — picks up the phone or walks in the door. And, this important experience doesn't end until long after the product has been delivered. In fact it never ends!

Here's another profound truth: Customers scrutinize how you treat them after the sale as much as they evaluate you while they are making a decision to buy. It is like you are under a magnifying glass. Customers are closely watching how you handle every situation. Remember: Everything counts when it comes to earning a customer's loyalty.

There are four specific things that customers say they will never forget about doing business with you:

1. Customers do not forget attitudes.

This includes the attitudes of everyone in your company that they deal with — the receptionist, the salesperson, even the driver or messenger who delivered the product to their office. Each member of your corporate team is an extension of the customer service experience. And, any person involved in this chain of events who has a sour attitude or doesn't care about customer service will spoil the whole experience for your customer.

> Any person involved in this chain of events who has a sour attitude or doesn't care about customer service will spoil the whole experience for your customer.

I want to work with people who have a "no matter what" attitude. No matter what it takes we will find solutions together. The good news is that customers also remember the people who are pleasant to work with. Here's what a friend of mine had to say on this topic: "I made a personal decision many years ago that I would only do business with nice people. I make a conscious decision to seek nice people. And, most of the time, the way I judge nice people is by the way they treat members of my staff."

Life is too short to deal with unpleasant people…more than once.

2. Customers do not forget your promises.
Our business is based on trust. When you lose a customer's trust, there is really no basis for continuing the business relationship.

Life is too short to deal with unpleasant people …more than once.

The fine print written in contracts, proposals, and brochures is great for lawyers, but what you say is far more powerful than your product brochure or contract. Customers do not have the time or desire to double-check all of your statements; they need to trust you for that information.

Just keep everything plain and simple. No pie in the sky promises. Earn your customer's trust and their business all at the same time.

3. Customers do not forget how you handle any issues or misunderstandings. There is another chapter in this book addressing problem solving, but be aware that an issue or problem is always an opportunity for your customer to remember the professional way you handled an uncomfortable situation. In fact, when we have an issue or misunderstanding we have an opportunity to develop a bonded relationship more than any other time.

When those misunderstandings occur, you might think your customer has no clue about your recommendation. You may be right. But, as one person requested, "Just allow me to be dumb with dignity. When I do not see things your way, don't attack me. Communicate with me. Most of the time you will discover that even though my

> When we have an issue or misunderstanding we have an opportunity to develop a bonded relationship more than any other time.

position may be dumb in your mind, there is a logical reason why I feel that way. Allow me the dignity to explain my point of view."

4. **Customers do not forget what happens after the sale.** The best marketing tool available to you is your customer's satisfaction after the sale. You can really set yourself apart by becoming an after-the-sale customer champion. Many times I have more business to give and will be glad to give it to you...if you earn it.

And this is not rocket science — you can earn my future business by remembering what some refer to as "the small stuff." Believe it or not, customer service personnel often forget "small stuff," like my company's name or operating protocol. Yes, some of my vendors cannot even remember my name when it is time to fill out the contract.

That's silly, you say? I agree. Think how you could stand out by remembering a customer's birthday, their interests and something about their family members, i.e., new grandkids, wife's recent surgery, etc. Jot these seemingly "silly" facts into your electronic organizer. Don't make it complicated...because it's not!

Your company is evaluated continually by your customers and even by third party services on the Internet. Your customers will become loyal to you if your customer service team develops a "no matter what" attitude, keeps their promises, quickly addresses issues, and takes care of the customer after the sale.

Remember: Everything Counts!

It's All in the Attitude!

A man dining at an Italian restaurant on New York's Mulberry Street told the owner, "Your veal parmagiana is better than the one I had in Rome last month."

"Of course it is," replied the owner. "They use domestic cheese. Ours is imported."

LISTEN UP!

Attack Issues Now!

A diamond is a chunk of coal that

made good under pressure.

—Anonymous

Your customers can deal with small problems. You may be surprised to know that customers even expect issues — or simply misunderstandings — to occasionally surface. That's just part of doing business. But, what customers have difficulty accepting are surprises! And, by 'surprises,' we mean situations that could have been eliminated or avoided if you had been proactive in addressing the issues.

Follow me on this. It is important!

There is a problem-solving rule called the 1-10-100 rule or you could call it the *molehills-to-mountains rule.*

Loosely translated, the rule states that the longer a problem exists without being identified or addressed, the more expensive and time consuming the problem is to fix.

You can see the molehills-to-mountains rule happening in almost every organization. It could be a billing discrepancy, quality issue, or lack of communication. Here is an example of how your expense escalates the longer a problem is allowed to exist:

> The longer a problem exists without being identified or addressed, the more expensive and time consuming the problem is to fix.

Let's suppose that there is a quality problem with a product. Imagine that some automobile tires are manufactured with a defect. The defect is discovered in the assembly line at the manufacturing plant. Let's say it would cost a dollar to stop the assembly line, reengineer the tire and fix the problem at that point. We now have a **$1 molehill.** However, for whatever reason, the decision is made to ignore the defect and allow the tires to be shipped to the dealer.

The dealer receives the tire and recognizes the defect with the tire. If the dealer sends the tire back to the manufacturer, it will now cost the manufacturer about $10 (because of shipping cost, rework, dealer time, etc.) to resolve the problem he could have solved originally for $1. The $1 molehill is now a **$10 hill.**

Suppose that the dealer chooses to ignore the problem and sells the tire to a customer. The customer discovers the problem and returns the tire to the dealer for replacement. The cost of replacing the tire at that point could be $100 or more — okay, much, much more!

In this case, the dealer and manufacturer could lose the customer, the customer could sue the tire company or, an accident could be attributed to the faulty tire, resulting in millions of dollars of negative publicity, litigation, etc. Now, the $1 molehill has now become a **$100+ mountain!**

An example such as this could lead to a potential disaster for your company.

The molehill-to-mountain rule is true, almost without exception: The longer a situation is allowed to exist, the more costly it will be to fix. Very seldom, if ever, does a problem solve itself and simply go away.

> Very seldom, if ever, does a problem solve itself and simply go away.

I once heard an old saying: "Never leave a nail sticking up where you find it." When you apply this old proverb to corporate America today, the translation is: Attack issues as they come up!

Another important point while we're on this subject: Problem-solving is not figuring out where to pass the buck. Your customers are not interested in finding out who to blame. Just resolve the issue and do it quickly — before it becomes an even greater issue.

And you can take this to the bank — most of the time, the biggest dilemma you'll face is poor communication. This is usually the result of not taking the time to understand or be understood. There is absolutely no need for us to fall into that trap in our customer/supplier relationship. If an issue arises let's work together to solve it before it becomes a major problem for either of us!

> Most of the time, the biggest dilemma you'll face is poor communication.

Listen up! Here's what one of my customers told me: "Even if I am your customer, I am not always right. I am probably right about the same amount of time that you are right, but, in the long run, does it really matter who is right? When a problem arises, just keep your cool. Listen to what I need, provide me with some alternatives and help me to feel good about the solution we come up with together." That is some pretty good advice.

The Golden Package

Jim Barksdale, former COO of FedEx, created a customer service philosophy that every package should be treated as the customer's golden package — the package that could make or break their business. Out of the millions of packages that FedEx picked up, sorted and delivered, FedEx employees were to treat every one as though it was the most important package in the world. The golden package mindset was a significant factor in FedEx becoming one of the most reliable service companies in the world.

Give Me Lagniappe

Always do more than is required of you.
— General George S. Patton

Lagniappe (lan-yap) may be a new term to you but, whether it is new to you or not, it is important to your customer. Lagniappe is a French word for "a little something extra or an unexpected gift." Many years ago, Louisiana French storeowners used lagniappe as a reward to attract and keep their customers. They had already discovered the value of customer loyalty.

For example, if a customer ordered five pounds of sugar, the clerk would dish out five pounds on the scale and then, with a smile, add an additional measure and say "lagniappe." That was the storeowner's way of adding a little extra value and saying that your business was important.

Basically, what they were really doing was under-promising and over-delivering. Who knows, maybe that extra measure was actually rolled into the price, but the perception was that the customer was receiving a little something extra, plus they saw in the eyes of the storeowner that their business was appreciated. How could the customer not smile back when the storeowner just gave them more than their expectations and smiled while uttering the word "lagniappe?"

> The customer was receiving a little something extra, plus they saw in the eyes of the storeowner that their business was appreciated.

Don't you think that customer walked away feeling good about doing business with the Creole shopkeeper? You bet they did!

My point is simply this: **Customers enjoy positive surprises.** In fact, my most memorable experiences, good and bad, are things that happened randomly and unexpectedly. Who doesn't enjoy receiving a little something extra over and above their expectations? Who doesn't appreciate a little extra help? And, my rule of reciprocity is that when I enjoy doing business with you, I will spend more money.

That is a pretty simple formula for customer service success, isn't it? Deliver what you promise — add a little something extra, make my experience enjoyable and I will spend more money with you.

But, here is the catch...before lagniappe can be added, you have to understand what your customers expect from you...and remember...the game has changed!

Think about the experience of filling a prescription. In the past, you would go to the local drug store, turn in your prescription, carry on a conversation with the pharmacist and walk away with your medicine. That was what you expected, received, and what you were willing to pay for. The lagniappe was the personal interaction.

> Add a little something extra, make my experience enjoyable and I will spend more money with you.

Today, not many pharmacists are available to carry on a personal conversation. Your choices are different. You could go to your local grocery/drug store, stand in line for 20 minutes and are usually ignored and rarely recognized. You become frustrated, turn in the prescription and wait another 20 minutes for the medicine. Or, without leaving your house, you can dial up an online pharmacist, listen to Muzak for 45 seconds, punch in your order using your telephone buttons and have it delivered to your house tomorrow.

You see, without a relationship with the pharmacist, there is really no good reason to keep doing business the traditional way. The value that personalized customer service should be adding is actually preventing a pleasant experience. Instead of lagniappe, I am getting less and less of what I expected.

So, what do I — the client — expect from you, the vendor?

In a nutshell, I expect you to pay attention to my expectations, deliver

> Pay attention to my expectations, deliver on your promises and add lagniappe.

on your promises and add lagniappe. Get creative with the lagniappe — it doesn't have to be clever, expensive or time consuming. Just add a little something extra.

Lagniappe Examples

Southwest Airlines – *Donuts and coffee*

Marriott Hotels – *Juice and Fruit*

Olive Garden – *Breadsticks*

Lands' End – *No questions asked return policy*

Doubletree Hotels – *Hot cookies*

ClubCorp Country Clubs – *Personal greeting of member four times each visit.*

BMW – *Return cars sparkling clean from routine service.*

FedEx – *Free computer for shipping and tracking*

Discount Tire – *Rotate tires and fix flats free*

LISTEN UP!

Get Wired

Take all the swift advantage of the hours.
— William Shakespeare

Here is your challenge. Your competition is no longer just the other person down the street. In fact, besides the familiar competitors, the new wave of competition now consists of a mouse, keyboard, monitor, and the "Enter" button.

I have been a little slow, climbing aboard the e-commerce train but more and more of my decisions are being based on what I read on my computer screen. My boss is pressuring me to expand my knowledge base and save our company money by buying from anybody, anywhere and at any time. She says that every business is affected by this electronic commerce change. People are buying computers, cars, houses, pictures, books, office machines, industrial equipment, stocks, real estate, insurance, and even airplanes over the Internet. No one is immune to the change, not me, not you and definitely not your company.

And, your company — whether you're full-fledged online or not — is also being evaluated by third-party companies on the web. Based on your performance and input from clients, your company is being judged on its customer service, its products and its management strategies. Yes, the Internet has changed our entire world and how we do business.

The days of Willy Loman walking door to door are just a memory. Yet, the days of ordering everything without interacting with a human being have not yet arrived, either, and all ordering may never be totally electronic. But, we both have to admit the game has changed!

> **We both have to admit the game has changed!**

All $400 billion of products purchased electronically this year are purchased outside the traditional sales and customer service channels. $400 billion! Think about it. That's a big chunk of business for someone to lose.

But, here's the good news. Yes, the game has changed but the opportunities for you to earn my business have increased—not decreased. You see, more than ever, I want — no, I need extraordinary customer service.

One of the changes in this game is how fast and accurately I receive information before making any decisions. You have to get on board the technology train to help me do that! What I really need is real-time information available to me, day and night.

> The opportunities for you to earn my business have increased—not decreased.

Okay, I hear you saying, "Oh no! You want total accessibility to me wherever I am, whatever I am doing?"

Not exactly. I want you to be available through instant accessibility of information, which does not have to come from you, personally. In fact, many of my calls to you could be avoided if I knew where to get the information. This would save both of us time.

Why not create your own personal, or even departmental, domain and web site? Then, use it to address the majority of my questions. Need a starting point? Here are the five areas that I would want to access at my convenience:

1. **Access to your company's resumé.** What credentials do you have to earn the right to my business? I would like to know your company's mission, vision and values. Yes, values. I want to work with people and companies who walk and talk about the importance of customers like me. I like to know as much about the company I am buying from as I need to know about the product that I am buying.

2. What about your product? This information was on the brochure that I misplaced. What is your customer satisfaction ranking and how is it measured? What are your guarantees? What is your market share and what separates you from your competition? Would you publish a list of referrals and current clients with titles and telephone numbers? Don't forget — this area should also show the features and benefits of your product.

3. What about your people? This is another area to which I would like instant accessibility. I'd like to know as much as possible about the people you will provide as my support team. Pictures would be great. I enjoy seeing the faces of people I talk to. It makes it more personal and less confrontational. By providing the information of who to call when I need instant access would eliminate wasting your time.

> I'd like to know as much as possible about the people you will provide as my support team.

4. What are others saying about your company? The fourth area on your web site should contain any articles that have been published about your company or your product. I know, I know. You have sent me numerous past articles, but I do not have the time to search my files for that information. A portion of your web site containing this information is much more user-friendly.

5. What I can expect from you? No, not what I
can expect from your company! I want to know what
I can expect from you, my customer service rep. How
often will you communicate with me? How often will
we have an account review? How quickly should I
expect you to return phone calls? How much time is
required to settle a pricing dispute?

You see, I just need to know what to expect. Putting
everything in writing clarifies our expectations for each
other and then we can hold each other accountable.

So, this so-called "technology threat" can actually be
used to your advantage. Get on board so my decision to
keep buying from you will reduce my risks and keep us
both happy.

Well-Intended Customer Service

Robert Dedman, founder of ClubCorp — the largest owner and operator of country clubs in the world, tells a story of how customer service expectations can sometimes be misinterpreted.

Mr. Dedman initiated a customer service program that focused on employees knowing every member of the club and calling the member by name at least four times each visit. The purpose was to create a warm and friendly atmosphere for the members.

Shortly after the initiative, Mr. Dedman visited the Lancer Club in San Francisco with a guest. One of the newer employees, trying to impress the founder of ClubCorp went over to take their drink order.

As he approached the table, he said, "Mr. Dedman, Mr. Dedman, Mr. Dedman, Mr. Dedman, what would you and your guest like today?"

LISTEN UP!

Be Profitable

The law of competition is best for the

race because it insures survival of the fittest.

— Andrew Carnegie

One advantage of the new electronic commerce arena is that the customer is not placed in an adversarial role with customer service. You cannot argue, insult or hurt the feelings of an electronic order. What you see is what you get and sometimes that is not all bad. But, most of the time I find this a rather empty experience.

For instance, I don't enjoy making decisions with a machine that does not understand my company's process and the impact my decisions may make on others. You see, working with someone like you reduces my risks and should make us both happy.

A business partnership is a two-way street. My job is to create value for my company. That value may come from lowering costs or improving processes or eliminating waste. Your job is to create value for my company as well. We are not adversaries; we have the same goals. You help me create value for my company and I will reward you with more business. It is as simple as that.

> You help me create value for my company and I will reward you with more business.

Now, I also want you to make a profit.
Surprised? Remember we are on the same team, a team that specializes in creating value. You have to make a profit to stay in the game. And, from my perspective, there is a direct correlation between delivering outstanding customer service and maintaining a profitable company. I have seen numerous companies with good products go out of business because they did not know how to take care of their customers.

> From my perspective, there is a direct correlation between delivering outstanding customer service and maintaining a profitable company.

The worst thing that could happen is for me to invest my time and energy in our business relationship and, suddenly you go out of business. That's a terribly painful scenario for everybody.

One of the elements that I bring to the relationship is profit for you. You cannot survive without profit and I cannot survive without a product similar to your product. But, you must know, up front, that the profit you gain from me will be earned. I will be glad to help you achieve all of your goals but profit is not free!

Here is how to earn profit while helping me create value for my company:

You have to know my business if you expect to help me create value.
I expect you to be a business consultant and a long-term ally. Building relationships take time. Spend our time wisely by being focused and listening while we are together. You cannot create value for me if you do not know the impact your product or service will have on my business. I assure you . . . the more you learn about my business, the more you will earn from my business.

> The more you learn about my business, the more you will earn from my business.

Respect the process.
I am aware that you may have a quota to achieve. I will help you make your quota if you don't push me into making a decision before I have completed my decision-making process. Your job is to provide timely information so that I can speed up the sales cycle. Remember, I seldom want to be sold, but I always want to buy!

When all the information that I need has been provided, give me some room to create the right timing for us to develop additional value for my company.

Create value by providing several alternatives.
Your ability to propose different alternatives is another thing that separates you from the e-commerce world. You can think with emotion and logic. I need you to provide alternatives that will improve my decisions.

A profitable partnership! Creating value for my company by understanding my business, respecting the sales process, and providing alternatives. That is the beginning of a long-term, loyal relationship.

U.S. Office of Consumer Affairs Findings

Jan

✓ For every unsatisfied customer who complains, 26 other unhappy customers say nothing. And of those 26, 24 won't come back.

✓ The average customer who experienced a problem with an organization tells 9 or 10 people about it.

✓ Of the customers who register a complaint, between 54 percent and 70 percent will do business again with the organization if their complaint is resolved. That figure goes up to a staggering 95% if the customer feels that the complaint was resolved quickly.

LISTEN UP!

Check Up!

There's always room for improvement.

It's the biggest room in the house.

— *Louise Heath Leber*

This book has been written from the perspective of a customer who cares enough to tell you the truth. Unfortunately, many of your customers will walk away from doing business with your company without saying a word. In fact, on average, United States corporations lose almost half of their customers every five years. In addition, U.S. companies will lose half of their employees in four years. Coincidence? Maybe...but probably not!

A better answer may be that customer loyalty begins with employee loyalty. Loyal customers are built through years of building relationships. If employee turnover is so rampant in your company that relationships cannot be built with your customers, you can expect to continue to see customers walk.

I am not fond of going to the doctor for a checkup. In fact, I hate it. Even before I arrive at the office, I am anxious that the doctor may find something that I do not want to know. But, I also know that the sooner a problem is discovered, the better my chances are to overcome the problem and get on with a healthy life.

Your business is no different. If you chose to ignore the voices and actions of your customers, the long-term health of your business is in jeopardy.

On the next page are 15 questions for you to complete in a customer service checkup. Answer all the questions as honestly as you can. Next, ask your staff and customers to do the same. This will show you if there are any gaps between your perceptions and those of your customers and staff.

> If you chose to ignore the voices and actions of your customers, the long-term health of your business is in jeopardy.

The CornerStone Customer Service Self-Test

1–never; 2–rarely; 3–sometimes; 4–frequently; 5–always

_____ 1. Our company is totally committed to creating satisfied customers.

_____ 2. We use technology to assist our customers in their decision-making process.

_____ 3. Serving customer needs takes precedence over our internal needs.

_____ 4. Each person in our company talks to customers at least weekly.

_____ 5. We add lagniappe to our customer's buying experience.

_____ 6. We deliver what we promise to our customers.

_____ 7. We actively seek customer complaints.

_____ 8. We eliminate unnecessary procedures that do not add value for our customers.

_____ 9. We clearly understand what our customers expect from our company.

_____ 10. We consistently show our customers that we care about their business.

_____ 11. Our employees are experts in the products we sell.

_____ 12. We treat our employees with dignity and respect.

_____ 13. We communicate frequently with our customers.

_____ 14. We study our competitors to get ideas on how we can do things better.

_____ 15. We reward customer loyalty.

Scoring:

60-75   **Great Job!** Your company is a customer service champion.

45-59   **Not Bad!** It may be a good time to refine your customer service skills.

30-44   **Watch Out!** You need to work on your customer service philosophy.

15-29   **Warning!** You are at risk of losing your customers.

Customer loyalty is not something that you can manufacture, buy, or invent. Delivering service excellence over and above the customer's expectations and doing it often is how you earn customer loyalty.

> Customer loyalty is not something that you can manufacture, buy, or invent.

If you take care of your customers, they will take care of your business.

It is as simple as that!

A Customer

A customer is the most important visitor on our premises. He is not dependent on us — we are dependent on him. He is not an outsider in our business — he is part of it. We are not doing him a favor by serving him — he is doing us a favor by giving us the opportunity to do so."

—Author Unknown

David Cottrell, President and CEO of CornerStone Leadership, is an internationally known leadership consultant, seminar leader and speaker. His business experience includes senior management positions with Xerox and FedEx. He also led the successful turnaround of a chapter eleven company before founding CornerStone.

He is the author of *Birdies, Pars, & Bogies, Leadership Lessons from the Links, Leadership...Biblically Speaking, The Power of Principle-Based Leadership, 175 Ways to Get More Done in Less Time and Listen Up, Leader.*

He lives in DeSoto, Texas with his wife Karen and their children, Jennifer, Kimberly and Michael.

Mark C. Layton is Chairman, President and Chief Executive Officer of PFSweb Inc. (Nasdaq: PFSW), a leading Internet logistics provider headquartered in Plano, Texas.

Layton, a 1981 graduate of Northern Arizona University is a recognized leader in the utilization of technology in business. He is a highly sought public speaker on issues including electronic commerce, leadership, technology trends, supply chain management, web enabled call centers, financial management, and Christian principals in business.

Mr. Layton is the co-author of *175 Ways to Get More Done in Less Time and is the author of .coms or .bombs...Strategies for profit in e-Business.*

CornerStone Leadership Retreats, Keynotes and Workshops

Invite David Cottrell to speak at your next leadership retreat or management workshop. David is a dynamic, fast moving, and entertaining speaker whose presentation will reinforce your corporate objectives.

A partial list of keynote and workshop clients include:

American Airlines • Cigna Healthcare • Cleveland Clinic
ClubCorp, International • Daisytek, International
Duke Energy • Ericsson, Inc. • Exxon • FedEx
Jostens Inc. • Lands' End • Professional Services Inc.
Ronstad International • Shoney's Restaurants
Southwestern Bell • State of Illinois
The Associates • The Kettle Restaurants

For additional information call 1-888-789-5323.

Other CornerStone Books:

Birdies, Pars, & Bogies: Leadership Lessons from the Links. A great gift for the golfing executive, golf tournament, and management retreats. Paperback $12.95.

Leadership...Biblically Speaking: The Power of Principle-Based Leadership. A guide on how to apply the leadership lessons from the bible to today's leadership challenges. Hardcover $17.95.

Listen Up Leader!: Ever wonder what employees think about their leaders? This book tells you the seven characteristics of leadership that people will follow. Soft cover $7.95.

175 Ways to Get More Done in Less Time: 175 really, really good suggestions that will help you get things done faster...and usually better. Soft cover $7.95.

CornerStone Trial Pack: Order four CornerStone publications for one low price! $39.95 (retail value of $46.80).

Books are available at amazon.com or call 1-888-789-lead (5323)

☑ Yes, please send me extra copies of

Listen Up, Customer Service!

Quantity	1-99	100-999	1,000-4,999	5,000+
Price Each	$8.95	$7.95	$6.95	$5.95

Listen Up Customer Service!	_____	copies	X	$ _____	=	$ _____
Trial Pack	_____	packs	X	$ $39.95	=	$ _____
175 Ways To Get More Done In Less Time	_____	copies	X	$ $7.95	=	$ _____
Listen Up, Leader	_____	copies	X	$ $7.95	=	$ _____
Birdies, Pars, & Bogies	_____	copies	X	$ $12.95	=	$ _____
Leadership…Biblically Speaking	_____	copies	X	$ $17.95	=	$ _____

Shipping and Handing	$ _____
Subtotal	$ _____
Sales Tax (8.25%-Texas Only)	$ _____
Total (U.S Dollars Only)	$ _____

SHIPPING AND HANDLING CHARGES

Total $ Amount	Up to $99	$100-$249	$250-$1199	$1200-$3000	$3000+
Charge	$8	$16	$30	$80	$125

NAME _____ JOB TITLE _____

ORGANIZATION_____ PHONE _____

SHIPPING ADDRESS_____ FAX _____

BILLING ADDRESS _____ EMAIL _____

CITY _____ STATE _____ ZIP _____

❏ PLEASE INVOICE (ORDERS OVER $200) PURCHASE ORDER NUMBER (IF APPLICABLE)

CHARGE YOUR ORDER: ❏ MASTERCARD ❏ VISA ❏ AMERICAN EXPRESS

CREDIT CARD NUMBER _____ EXP. DATE _____

SIGNATURE _____

❏ CHECK ENCLOSED (PAYABLE TO CORNERSTONE LEADERSHIP)
❏ I AM INTERESTED IN LEARNING MORE ABOUT THE CORNERSTONE LEADERSHIP PROGRAMS

FAX	**Mail**	**Web**	**Phone**
972.274.2884	P.O. Box 764087 Dallas, Texas 75376	www.cornerstoneleadership.com	888.789-LEAD

43